SELF - PUBLISHING 101

Learn valuable tools, tips and techniques used
By successful publishers

Darrell Mitchell II

DM Ink Publishing

Copyright © 2020 Darrell Mitchell II

Self - Publishing 101
Published by DM Ink Publishing
Los Angeles, CA
www.DMThePoet.com
678-871-0818
Copyright ©2020 by Darrell Mitchell II

This book or parts thereof may not be reproduced in any form, stored in a retrieval system, or transmitted in any form by any means - electronic, mechanical, photocopy, recording, or otherwise, except as permitted under sections 107 or 108 of the United States Copyright Act, without prior written permission of the following publishing party.
All Rights reserved

This book is dedicated to:
My children: Macayla, Maceo, Siara and Mavi'e, Thank you for support and the encouragement you have shown me and most importantly, the love that helps me overcome the battles we go through in life. A strong family foundation is the most important thing you can have in your life and I'm grateful for the one God has blessed me with.

CONTENTS

Title Page	1
Copyright	2
Dedication	3
Introduction	7
Business Entity Options	9
Proprietorship	10
Business Name	11
The Book Title	12
Misleading Titles	14
"Soft" Title and "Strong" Title	15
Font/Type Size	16
Interior	17
Design Your Book	18
Graphic Designer/Illustrator	19
Conventional/Traditional Printers	20
Print on Demand	22
Website Essentials	25
The cost for website development	26
Preparing Manuscripts	27

Preparing Illustrations	29
Preparing Photographs	30
Preparing Artwork	31
Tips for easing the page design process	33
Copy Editor	34
Story Editor	35
Pricing Your Book	37
Book Credentials	39
How to add your book with My Identifiers.com	41
How to register your copyright	43
Instructions for Applying to the Library of Congress	44
Publishing Books for Other Authors	45
About The Author	47

INTRODUCTION

Congratulations on purchasing a copy of "Self - Publishing 101"

In the ever changing fast paced industry of book publishing, factors like technology, business growth and market saturation creates a sea of unanswered questions and with even more answers. Many entrepreneurs and aspiring writers around the world want to know how to write, self-publish a book or build their own publishing company.

This book will equip you with the valuable tools, tips and techniques used by successful publishers. With over fifteen years of publishing experience I have been fortunate to write and publish over twenty books, assist sign and publish for six authors, and build and manage two publishing companies.

For years I also served as Vice President for my mentors publishing company, hosted writing workshops and conferences throughout Southern California and Atlanta, Georgia. This book will highlight the important steps needed to develop and manage a successful publishing company and produce and market quality books.

BUSINESS ENTITY OPTIONS

First things first is the legal business entity aspect of your company. The foundation of how your infrastructure is established is very important when you are investing in intellectual content. Especially when it comes to registering your products with ascap, the library of congress or receiving royalties for those best sellers you are going to release.

The structure will depend on your goal, your business partners and the market you plan to develop your books for. Being that we will be diving into the deep sea of rules and regulations, taxes, and copyright laws we will stay surface level on certain aspects to avoid getting lost in a rabbit hole of information. Let's start by covering the main business entity structure options:

PROPRIETORSHIP

- You are the sole owner of the business. You wear all the hats; you make all the decisions and have all the responsibility and liability.

Corporation

- A corporation has a chief officer (President), a financial officer and usually that person is the treasure. It also has a secretary and a board of directors.

- A corporation submits articles of incorporation to the secretary of state and the state must approve the corporation.

- When sued the plaintiff can only attach the assets owned by the corporation.

Partnership

- Consist of two or more partners.

- Partners decide who will manage the business.

- Each partner has an assigned responsibility, or you may have a silent partner one who invest money into the business but has no input on the daily operation of the business.

- Each partner may have their personal assets jeopardized when a judgment is placed on the partnership business.

BUSINESS NAME

- A business name is a marketing component.
- It is a branding component.
- It should signify what business you are in.
- It should also tell the public what service you provide.

Examples

- BB's Enterprise. This name does not give any indication of the type of business you are in or the services you provide.
- BB's Publication. This name could suggest to some that you operate a magazine, newspaper, or other publication. However, it is not clear.
- BB's Publishing House. This name indicates that you are a publishing company.
- BB's Publishing This name also indicates that you are in the publishing business.

THE BOOK TITLE

- The title is very important. It should lend itself to what the book is about.

- It should not be misleading, people want to know what they are purchasing, and the title will give them a clue.

Subtitles

- Sometimes, it's necessary to use a subtitle to give further clues about what your book is about. If you have the word "novel" on your front cover, it's made clear that your book is a fictional work, regardless of the title.

For example: the book, Swift Board King, has a subtitle: Spending Pennies And Skating Like A Pro.

- This sub-title helps the reader to get a clue as to what's in the book. The title of your book will indicate the genre: Poetry, fiction, non-fiction, autobiography, self-help, a children's book, etc. Content assumption, assumptive title is when a conclusion drawn about what the book is about from the title and, in most cases, the assumption is wrong. Oftentimes a customer will not purchase the book because their assumption of what the book is about is totally incorrect. There are cases where a person has purchased a book and returned it because the title was misleading.

MISLEADING TITLES

Example:
A Strawberry girl in a Pineapple world

- This title will lead one to think that it is an autobiography. This title is a book of poetry and prose, therefore the title is misleading. The title should be: A Strawberry girl in a pineapple world: [with a subtitle] A collection of poetry and prose.

"SOFT" TITLE AND "STRONG" TITLE

- A strong title grabs the reader's attention more quickly. A soft title is one the reader has to look at many times before feeling compelled to pick it up.

Soft title:
"What every daughter needs from her father".
Strong title:
"Fatherless women: [with a subtitle] What every daughter needs from her father"

FONT/TYPE SIZE

- Your book should be easy to read

- A 12 font size is easy on the eye. Never make the font larger in order to increase your page count.

- Too large of a font is as hard on the ye as a font that is too small.

- Do not type your book in all capital letters.

- A good, seasoned formatter can get you the page count you desire without making the font size extra-large to do so.

INTERIOR
Layout/Design

- Formatting your book in an appropriate style according to the genre.

- Designing a style to your book.

- Selecting a special way to introduce each new chapter, page numbers, headings, spacing, indentations/paragraphs, quotes, references, citations, footnotes/ endnotes, indexes, and more.

- A good book designer/formatter makes a great difference.

DESIGN YOUR BOOK

Many hand out their banner far too soon as a desktop publisher, book designer and formatter. Some think all a formatter needs to know is how to set the margins for a book's trim size (i.e., 5.5 x 8.5, 6 x 9, etc.).

- There is much to know about How to choose a formatter to design your book and about professionally formatting a book. Different nook types and genres need a special/unique look and personality. A book on finance would have a different personality than a fiction book. The best way to choose a formatter is by a referral from someone who has used the service and is satisfied with their work. The formatter should have samples of its work posted on its web site. If not, ask for samples. Furthermore, ask for a sample interior layout for your book before they begin work on your book. Go to a bookstore and look at different types of books and different layouts designs/styles.

GRAPHIC DESIGNER/ ILLUSTRATOR

It's always best to have a sense of what you are looking for in a book cover and for illustrations. It's a good idea to spend extra time with the illustrator so that you two can have a clear understanding of the vision for the project.

- Please know that if you continue to change the concept that you presented to the illustrator, he/she will have to charge you additional fees for your project.

- Illustrations are charged per illustration and each time you start over with the concept you are asking the illustrator to create something new. If you continue doing so, each character could become a new illustration versus a modification of a character. If you are not careful, the cost for your illustrations could easily double your anticipated cost.

CONVENTIONAL/ TRADITIONAL PRINTERS

- Conventional/Traditional Printers are printers who usually print large quantity of books, and the cost is based on your print run. However, some conventional printers are now printing short run on books also. Short-Run and print-on-demand have almost become the norm. Authors are no longer printing thousands of books and having them sit in their garages. They now create the demand for their books, and they print on demand, leveraging their finances.

- When using conventional printing and major distributors order books from you, you pay the printer to print your books. When a bookstore orders from a major distributor, the distributor will order the books from you. You must then ship the books to the distributor; you pay the shipping cost, and you give the distributors a 50%-65% discount because they give the bookstore a 40% discount on the books they purchase from the distributor. The distributor pays the author 90 days from purchase.

PRINT ON DEMAND

- You give the distributor a 40% discount and in 90 days the distributor will send you a check for 40% less the retail cost, less the printing fees, and you have incurred zero shipping cost. This is a great way to print and sell your books. You are leveraging your finances; You are not paying the high cost of shipping, and you are keeping more of the money from your book in your pocket.

- When using a conventional printer, the cost per book is higher unless printing large quantities (i.e., 500 to 1,00 books). In all situations, I prefer printing with print-on-demand, because:

    1.) I can order 1 to 1,000 books. After placing an order I can expect to receive my books within 7 to 10 days. The books are shipped from Tennessee via UPS Ground.

    2.) When a bookstore orders my books from Ingram Books, one of the largest book distributors, nationally and internationally. Lightning source prints the books, whether it is one of one hundred

SELF - PUBLISHING 101

books, Ingram will ship the book to the book seller and in 90 days they will pay the distributor (DM Ink Publishing) for books sold. Ingram will deduct their 40% discount plus the printing charge and send a check for the difference to the author publisher.

3.) I only have to pay up-front (out of pocket for the books that I am going to sell myself. Books ordered by the bookstore/wholesalers are printed by Lighting Source Printing, and the printing charge is deducted form my royalty statement when Ingram pays me for my books in 90 days.

4.) Even when you order a large quantity of books from a conventional printer and get a $2.00 to $3.00 less cost per book via doing so, the bottom line in the profits is extremely less. Ingram will order the book from the author/publisher, and they want a 60% discount on the books ordered. Ingram requires that the author/publisher, incur the shipping charge (shipping charge is very expensive).

You will incur all shipping charges, and Ingram has a return policy, books can
Be returned as long as the title is in print. You prepay the shipping, and have to wait 90 days plus to get paid for your books.

- Let's say that you printed via conventional

printer, and the book cost is $2.00 to $3.00 cheaper. Remember, Ingram will order the books from your distributor will have to incur the shipping charge. You have to pay for the printing cost in order to have books on-hand to sell to Ingram. Even when you save $2.00 to $3.00 on printing, it will cost you more than what you saved on printing form the shipping. Shipping includes, paying for boxes or envelopes to ship books in tape pallets to keep books from shifting, and your time for invoicing and going to the post office.

- When amazon order books from you, they get a 55% discount and you have to prepay the shipping charge. They pay in 60 to 90 days, and they may return books you too. When Barnes & Nobles order books from you, they get a 40% discount and you can add the shipping charge to their invoice. They pay within 60 days. Books are shipped to the store that placed the order, and you will bill their home office.

WEBSITE ESSENTIALS

The importance of having an eCommerce website

- With the internet, you can promote your book to book clubs, get permission from other sites to link to your website, or write articles for websites and mention your book as part of your book as part of your byline for the article.

THE COST FOR WEBSITE DEVELOPMENT

- You can develop an internet and website presence for less than $60 per month. To keep cost down and control your image, you should manage your own website.

- The fee for building a basic web site should be no more than $350.00 You do not need to pay a webmaster a consulting fee to have them teach you how to manage your site.

- Microsoft FrontPage and Dreamweaver are good program for building your website. With eCommerce, you make it possible for anyone to purchase your book from anywhere in the world.

PREPARING MANUSCRIPTS

- Type your book in Microsoft®Word.

- Use the same font throughout the whole book, preferably Times New Roman 12pt.

- It is important that all pages are aligned within the same margins throughout the books.

- Start each paragraph with a left indent using the tab key.

- Do not use the space bar to start a new paragraph Number each page starting with page one

- Do not press enter at the end of the line. The computer will automatically go to the next line and continue. Only press the enter key at the end of a paragraph, and this will start a new paragraph.

- Use italics for books, movies and magazine titles.

- Any word or sentence that you think should be emphasized, bold or italicize it.

- If you have special prayers or scriptures that you want to be set apart in the book, italicize the selection.

- Bold your titles and subtitles.

PREPARING ILLUSTRATIONS

Preparing illustrations, photos, artwork, line art, charts, maps, and diagrams-Your book may include one or more illustrations. It may cost extra to use illustrations, but they're almost always worth it. some types of books (a children's book, for example) are hard to imagine without illustrations.

PREPARING PHOTOGRAPHS

If you're going to use photos that have already been developed, the original photo print is the best source for scanning. Color photos can be rendered in black and white, but not the other way around. Your computer files of photos can be used if the quality is adequate. If you take pictures with a digital camera, read the directions carefully and don't include pictures that were taken with a resolution anything less than 300dpi.

- One (1) printed copy of your manuscript. The text should be printed on white, 8 1/2" X 11" ordinary bond paper. Print only on one (1) side of the paper.

- Submit the manuscript on a CD, DVD, Flash drive, or by E-mail.

PREPARING ARTWORK

- Provide original artwork, not copies, especially if its is color.

- Preparing Line Art. These are the drawings with no "grey scale" tones, just black lines on a white background.

- Send line art as "jpeg" or "TIFF" files with 300dpi resolutions.

- Preparing Charts and Diagrams. Often your graph or chart from Word or Excel will import into the typeset program without any problem.

- However , Illustrations must be constructed so that they will be consistent with the rest of the book.

- One (1) printed copy of your manuscript. The text should be printed on white, 8 1/2" X 11" ordinary bond paper. Print only on one (1) side of the paper.

- Submit the manuscript on a CD, DVD, Flash drive, or by E-mail

TIPS FOR EASING THE PAGE DESIGN PROCESS

- Carefully label photos and artwork.

- If you send photo or art by CD or DVD, scan photos or other art at 300 dpi resolution and send them as "jpeg" files.

- Send original art, not art that has been printed.

COPY EDITOR

The copy editor is mainly concerned with spelling, grammar, and sentence structure. This editor makes certain that all of your words are spelled correctly and that there is subject and verb agreement throughout the story. A good copy editor checks for sentence fragments, run-on sentences, or paragraphs that are too long, as well as makes sure that adjectives and adverbs are used sparingly and correctly.

STORY EDITOR

- The story editor is concerned with things such as: pacing (Does the story move along well? Does the reader have to reread to make sense of what is happening in the story?); character development (Can the reader connect with or "feel" the characters? Are the characters believable?).

- Are you telling the reader or are you showing the reader the drama? Can the reader feel what is happening? Does the read get caught up the story? Are you involving the emotion of your reader so that he/she will root for your main character? Are you using a compelling situation? Have you layered your plot and your subplots? Do you use stilted versus conversational dialogue? Do you introduce your back story too soon?

This is only the beginning. There is much more to what a story editor looks for when editing a novel, but the input of such a professional is incalculably valuable to any writer, whether it is their first novel or their tenth.

The story editor is also concerned with whether you are

introducing too many characters at the same time; conflict (Is conflict or tension introduced too early enough in the story?); Does the reader get a sense of tension building, and is the reader motivated to keep reading to see the resolution?); verb tense consistency (Is the writer consistent in the use of the present or past tense?); point of view (Is the story told in the first or third person? Is the story being told by the writer, a narrator, or the main character?).

A good story editor will help you use the art of Show vs. Tell. Do you have language dissonance regarding the type of characters that you are portraying? For example, do you have a scientist speaking in street talk, or street person speaking like a college professor? If you do, there should be a logical reason, such as the scientist who has pulled himself up by his bootstraps from the streets, or the street person who has self-educated himself. Do you plant a "MacGuffin"-which is a goal or desire or yearning, which will fuel the plot?

Are you telling the reader or are you showing the reader the drama? Can the reader feel what is happening? Does the read get caught up the story? Are you involving the emotion of your reader so that he/she will root for your main character? Are you using a compelling situation? Have you layered your plot and your subplots? Do you use stilted versus conversational dialogue? do you introduce your back
story too soon?

    This is only the beginning. There is much more to what a story editor looks for when editing a novel, but the input of such a professional is incalculably valuable to any writer, whether it is their first novel or their tenth.

PRICING YOUR BOOK

Here are a few pointers for pricing your book for profit. Number one
is that you cannot base your price on how much research and time you put into your book-the reader is not concerned about that and could care less.

1. You should go to bookstores and compare books that are similar to your book in genre and page count. It does not matter to the reader that you can only print a few copies and therefore your printing prices is very expensive and therefore you have to charge more to make a profit, again, the reader could care less about that.

2. When pricing your book you must consider the cost of printing, so search for the best professional printer. Take into consideration the distributions that you are going to utilize for distributing your books. Examine the discount each distributor expects form you such Ingram wants 60% discount with a return policy and with you paying the shipping cost when shipping them your books. Amazon.com requires a 555 discount; your have to pay for shipping to them with a return policy. When selling to bookstores including Barnes and Noble bookstores a 40% discount is required, they will pay for shipping.

3. When your books are printed by Ingram, you are

able to select the discount you want to offer and you can choose to not accept returns. Remember , when a book store orders your books from Ingram Books, if Lighting, you do not incur the shipping charge. Lightning Source will pay you in 90 days, they will deduct from the retail price the percentage of discount that you offer them and the printing cost and they will send you the balance.

    4. When a retail customer orders your book you are getting paid the retail cost and the customer are paying the shipping cost. When counting the cost of shipping consider, envelopes, boxes, labels, tape and pellets to pack the book with.

    5. When pricing consider that you are not a celebrity writer and you are not a national known writer. So don't try to make a living off of just one book you can get there but it takes time

    6. When pricing your book consider that the retailer, sales tax is added to the book cost and shipping cost. Therefore would you rather make $5.00 per book from the sale of 1,000 books or $7-10 dollars for the sale from 200 books?

BOOK CREDENTIALS

Setting up your book for lightning Source, Inc.

About lightning source, Inc Lightning source,

Once. is connect with Ingram Book Group, the largest book distributor in the U.S.A., as well as internationally. Once your book is set up with Lightning Source, it is placed on Amazon.com and Barnes and Nobles.com web sites.

Once you have successfully completed your application and have received your approval email from lighting Source with your username and Password you can log on and go to How to set up your title, how to upload your files, and how to place an order. Just follow the steps for these procedures-they are simple instructions, now your're are ready.

How to Order You ISBN Numbers

- Log on to www.myidentifiers.com

- Click on the register button on the upper right hand side of the webpage. fill out the page as instructed.

- After you register with My Identifiers, choose a username and password.

- Then you can place your order for the number of ISBNs you want. 1 ISBN for $125.00, 10 ISBNs for $250.00

- Please remember your username and password.

HOW TO ADD YOUR BOOK WITH MY IDENTIFIERS.COM

(Books in Print)

What is MyIdentifiers.com?

MyIdentifiers.com provides publishers with tools and resources to purchase and assign book identifiers such as ISBNs, SANs, DOIs and others available through Identifiers Services.

MyIdentifiers.com provides a host of discover-ability services and solutions for publishers including automated tools to update or add to their title listing in Bowker's Books in Print and Global Books in Print databases.

Why should I register with MyIdentifierscom?

MyIdentifiers.com allows you to easily organize, communicate and market your book titles and optimize their discovery among a wide audience of book audio and video buyers. Bowker is the leading provider of bibliographic data your titles are exposed to many facets of the book industry through this single web application.

Once you find the right titles, Books in Print offers professional and patron list management tools to save title and streamline workflows. Connect-find favorite authors, genres, and purchase points Books in print is used every day by thousands of book professionals and library patrons to make connections connecting you to favorite authors and series; connecting genres.

7. Log On to www.myidentifiers.com

8. Click On, my Company link on the upper right hand corner of the page

9. On my company page, click on manage ISBNs Button

10. Then, Click on Assign Title Link

11. Follow These 4 Steps Below and complete Each Section

- Title & Cover
- Contributors (Authors)
- Format & size
- Sales & Pricing

HOW TO REGISTER YOUR COPYRIGHT

1. Log on to www.copyright.gov
2. On the homepage, look under how to register a work
3. The, Log on to eCO Link
4. Click On, under Click Here To Register link at the bottom of the left hand page
5. Complete the application form
6. Log on to www.copyright.gov
7. Online signup is $35.00, Register Through Mail is $65.00
8. Click on Register a Claim on the left hand side of the page,
9. follow Steps 1,2 and 3
10. Click The Start Registration Button
11. Click on Type of Work Button at the bottom of the Page and Select Literary Work
12. Note. don onto pre-register your work. This does not apply to you.
13. Do not click on Special Handling Section. There is a $760.00 charge
14. Click on Save for Later Button to save your information until you are ready to Pay for the Copyright.

INSTRUCTIONS FOR APPLYING TO THE LIBRARY OF CONGRESS

1. Log on to www.loc.gov/publish/pcn
2. to open up an account click on open an account underneath electronic PCN
3. Click on the application to participate link below the page
4. Complete the application as instructed
5. once you sing up with the library of congress, then keep your username and password for sage keeping.
6. Log on to www.loc.gov/publish/pcn
7. Click on the login link and then put in your username and password.
8. Click on PCN application on main menu page
9. Fill out your information as required.

PUBLISHING BOOKS FOR OTHER AUTHORS

1. Prepare a publishing contract

2. Prepare a book proposal cost contract and have the author to sign it

3. You should choose the editor, because the end result will reflect on your company. (It's a good idea to hire a proofreader to proof the book after the editor has finish. We all can have an oversight when editing Include $1.00-$1.50 per page for a proofreader. Make sure this is not the proofreader's first job. Get a referral.

4. After the book has been edited and proofread, have the author reread the manuscript. Have the author sign a form stating that he/she has read the edited manuscript and approved its readiness to go to the formatter. This is important because author, many times, seem to never book has been formatter,
changes could change the page pagination which could result in extra charges.

5. When you get back the galleys (proof pages of the fin-

ished book), read with the eye of an eagle before sending to the printer. Make sure the author clearly makes any corrections he/ she wants, using accepted proofreader's marks and a red pen. This is the appropriate time for the author to ensure his/her
message is being conveyed or if a word has been dropped, etc. However, do keep in mind that authors are so anxious to get that book "baby" in their hand they will rush through reading the galleys.

6. As the publisher, you should explain the importance of taking the extra time and reading their book, because in the end, the content will reflect positively or poorly on the author. But, this
not the time to add additional content and rewrite the book. Corrections are one thing and rewriting is another. There will be an extra charge when rewriting your book after the book has been formatted. In fact, the book should go back to the editor when there are major changes and rewrites, before sending back to the formatter.

7. When you get back to the galleys (proof pages of the finished book), read with the eye of an eagle before sending to the printer. Make sure the author clearly marks any corrections he/ she wants, using accepted proofreader's marks and a red pen.
This is the appropriate time for the author to ensure his/her message is being conveyed are so anxious to get that book in their hand they will rush through reading the galleys.

ABOUT THE AUTHOR

Darrell Mitchell

 DM Ink endeavors to encourage a generation to think better, write better and live better in life. As an organization we promote thinking on a creative level, and assist with various aspects of performing arts through fundraising events, showcases and community outreach programs. Our goal is to inspire, empower and enlighten the world through art and literature.

Our brand represents products that readers can easily relate to. The current catalog has built a solid foundation among readers and music enthusiast, who currently read and listens to inspirational, empowering and enlightening material. The spoken word poetry collection creates a connection with the reader. This collection also enlightens the reader and provides them with understanding. Each published piece is embedded with a message that challenges the reader to make a connection between ideas and concept's. More importantly, the series of poems give a testimony and explains how you can achieve your dreams by believing in them.

www.ingramcontent.com/pod-product-compliance
Lightning Source LLC
Chambersburg PA
CBHW070839220526
45466CB00002B/827